Shield

Lyndon Davies was born and brought up in Cardiff, but currently lives in Powys. His first collection of poems, *Hyphasis*, was published by Parthian in 2006. He co-runs the Glasfryn Seminars, a series of discussion groups on contemporary literature, and the Hay Poetry Jamboree, a yearly festival of innovative poetry.

Penny Hallas was born in Leeds, but now lives in Powys. She is a widely-exhibited freelance artist, painter, print maker, but also an art-therapist working in the NHS. Her artwork can be explored at www.penny.hallas.co.uk

Shield

Lyndon Davies

with illustrations by
Penny Hallas

Parthian
The Old Surgery
Napier Street
Cardigan
SA43 1ED
www.parthianbooks.co.uk

First published in 2010
© Lyndon Davies 2010
All Rights Reserved

Illustrations © Penny Hallas

ISBN: 978-1-906998-17-2

Editor: Norman Schwenk

Cover image © Penny Hallas
Cover design & typesetting by Lucy Llewellyn

Printed and bound by Dinefwr Press, Llandybïe

Published with the financial support of the Welsh Books Council.

British Library Cataloguing in Publication Data
A cataloguing record for this book is available from the British Library.

Contents

Prelude   1

Thaw   3

The Challenge   4

Hephaestus: A Passion   5

The Shield and the Muse   8

Beacon   11

Portrait of a Lady   12

Resistance (After Lucretius) 1   14

Tales of the Father   15

Clandestine   20

Diva   21

Anchorman – The Towers   23

Mappa   24

The Warrior Considers the Tulips   25

The Dream of the Sword   26

Punchinello's Egg   27

Strange Passage   29

Anchorman – Fire-Tunnel   30

Dancer   31

Petrifactive   33

Victims   34

The Warrior Considers the Real   35

Witness   37

Troubadour   38

Wanderer   39

The Fix   41

The Warrior and the Oak Trees   42

Resistance (After Lucretius) 2   43

Campanology   44

The Miner's Leader   45

The Wall   53

Anchorman – The Camps   54

Message from Ground Zero   56

The Guest   57

Dark   59

Hephaestus: The Forging   61

*There were five folds composing the shield
itself, and upon it he elaborated many things...*

The Iliad, *book 18, lines 481–482*
(Trans. Richmond Lattimore)

Shield

Prelude

Waiting, what are they waiting for?
Some wry convulsion; suddenly to be folded
each into the other, splat! like two globs
of dough,
when earth lifts its elbows and bears down
or sky hits the dyke?

Any combination
at all, of natural or man-made catastrophes;
or any one, or all combinations at once:
that is what they are waiting for,

out there on the killing-field,
the field that kills,
the brute field
where they have taken up their positions.

Thaw

The brook is hard now
and the grape a pebble
salting a man's hand;
clothes strike the rock,
defy it, temper it:
everything that was not
impervious to the hammer,
javelin, sword, curses,
impervious now as the blade turns, breaks
on its thrust, cold-shouldered
by warrior, by gleaner,
frays like a vapour-trail
under the high lamps
in the feast hall, a myth
beaten out by heels
in dust where the ox falls
in its time of yielding,
softening a girl's eye.

The Challenge

As one antagonist to another,
he said 'Come out and fight like a man;
come out, whoever you are, or I'll come and get you.'

But nothing moved and the shield just stood there
listening to itself, its looped plates
of varying metals doubling the light of stars
and bonfires,
its people going about their business.

Somehow he felt silly then, done up
in armour, in paint, but his feet ran on.
He lifted his sword to cut, his own shield
to parry,
but no-one was there but himself
on that field of dazzlements.
Then he heard a shout.

Hephaestus:
A Passion

Soft from the fall,
like a wad of bubble-gum
chewed by a supernova...

They giggled at me
in the disco: I wasn't
built for their pleasures.

Wherever I stepped
my feet stained the floor,
whatever I touched blackened.

All along the shore, too,
a five o'clock shadow
stubbled the tide-edge

when I bathed.
Embarrassment and unease
followed me everywhere.

Once a girl turned to me and a net
fell on my head.
I struggled but I couldn't get free.

She yawned and left.
I beat a faith
out of that,

beautiful but not to keep.
Never mind – that glimpse
blew the gates open.

And suddenly I saw
who I was: the fire
took my hand and shook it.

It stayed where I put it.
I fed it shapes,
it took what I gave it.

It would have mocked me, though,
given its own tongue,
the little that I knew.

Now I bend to the flames,
and toil away
and the mould closes over me –

hammering and quenching:
whatever I make
can never be passed on,

is made for the hand
that owns it, invulnerable
and unfriendly,

for that hand only.
Because I fell,
because I was cast out.

The Shield
and the Muse

1.
You can start here, or there, wherever
the fancy takes you, leave when you've had enough
or eyes flinch (that muddle, that glare). It's the tale
of a tale – fissures weaving up through the reredos
like the slow dance of a melancholy spider,
tropical nightmare plant. Everything
in its time – dagger, ghost... Sublime, the assenting
gape of the atrium. Hours pass, already
it's time to get up and you haven't even gone to bed,
or touched base. A ripple veers – it's the light,
you think, scattered threads of primrose and vermilion.
If she would only come, but she can't
while the cursor blinks, links proliferate. How
would she find her way? And who is she? Just someone
you saw in the coffee-aisle, scrutinising labels
as if she believed them, fingering the goods.

2.

From Parker's price guide for new and used cars
to ritual or not so ritual decapitation
is a hop and a click, a crick, is a frozen shoulder –
screen set back at an angle, the workbench
higher, you're alarmed to say, ergonomically
speaking, than good or lawful. But anyway
it hurts. Yes it hurts. What you have in mind
is love, though, not murder. Certainly you'd be advised
to follow those tendrils out through the backdrop –
mackerel clouds deploying as the dawn comes up
(no end to that flummery). As long as you're online
you can't *be*, that's how old-fashioned the set-up is
in this place. Forget regrets, flowers crushed
on the altar, a scent of somebody lying close,
their breath on the back of your hand – all of this
dissolves at the first touch, like knowledge. Is knowledge.

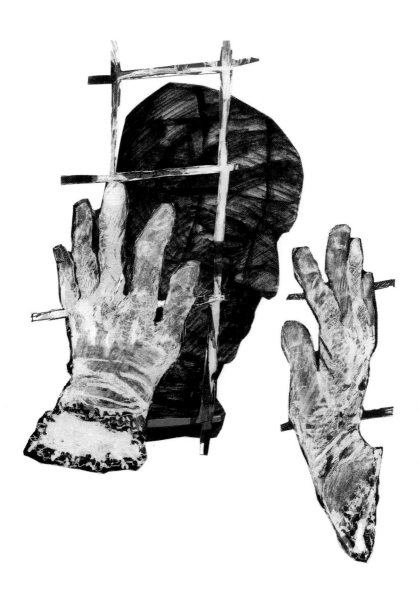

Beacon

As you turn towards me
I lift my head
just so, in the window,
opening a track –
a fine thread reeling down,
alight in the heather-tips,
in the shucked cusps
of water in the brooks;
keening out to summon you
back where your way ends,
wherever your way went.
As your steps approach
I lower my face
like a lamp going out:
your brow butts, your fingers
scrabble at the glass
like a blind man's
reading.

Portrait of a Lady

Clinched to her loss
at the table, the hard chair
upright, incommodious,
huddled with gripes, shoes
chiselling down into the patterns
quick with little dancing
japes: imbecilic hornpipe,
her fingers working
volume control, channel buttons,
none of them speak English
joined-up, the lamwidge
terrible, but still
they go on as her coy smile
evokes the glint under
histories of agglomerated
boredom. It's a shame
they're all actors, even
the actors are all actors.
One day a biscuit.
None of the food's hers
in cupboard, fridge, bin;
that's why she's as 'slim
as a wand'. Her egg takes
forever, but we don't mind,

Bruce Forsyth and I,
as the plots and the prospects sicken
over a daft planet
raddled with knife-crime
intruders and blonde people,
we have all evening.

Resistance
(After Lucretius) 1

You must understand – the originary bodies
falling like rain through the void, could never
of themselves have given impetus and shape
to anything in what we think of as world,
unless, at some point in their rapt descent,
some unpredictable moment, for no other reason
than that it is in their nature to do so,
they'd deviated by ever so small an extent,
the tiniest imaginable extent (since anything greater
would overtax our credulity). Collisions
engendered by many such slight eccentricities
of motion, demolishing the designs of fate,
give rise eventually to the whole shooting-match
of free-will and send you rushing out over the square,
the plough-land, the meadow, with violence in your heart.

Tales of the Father

1.
Excuse me if I watch
beside you, there are others.
This shadow is rich.
I thought I heard something
stir in the undergrowth.
The breeze? Something scuffling.
Perhaps a creature.
All around the perimeter
woven in good faith, with art, like a wreath –
eyes, minds straining out –
the lightning is gathering
low on the grass-stems,
in the high canopy
coiled or already pouncing. It's a good thing
I'm here: it's my forté.
Relax, let me take
the strain.
Where skin's broken I'll apply a mixture
of cod-liver oil and egg-whites.
When the spine snaps
it's a matter of maintenance.

Each morning I'll wake you
with a great fart, forgive me.
If you need anything,
just shout:
I can't promise to be sweet, but usually
you'll find me amenable.
I have my own worries.

2.
Lying here in the leaf-muck,
I can't help laughing at you
imperious in your cave
of fables – never quite
the innocent, unlike me
(this neverending clash
of pronouns); like me
when the jungle cracks
and light shaves the clearing,
ready to be up and at them,
marrow running thin
at sight of them, pulsing
out into the tracers,
with no-one between you
and the music: a fever
seguing into a bossa-nova.

3.
One day I rode
a horse through the ward.
It became a legend.
It may not have happened.

One day I leaned
on a tamarind tree
and a panther looked at me.

Shivering, shivering,
how far did I walk?
From Arakan to the Seven Giants,
following a naked lady

drawn on the pack
of the man in front of me.
Kindly,
lead kindly.

4.
I would like to praise you
and I will. If ever
you throw down the shield,
I will find it in me.

I promise you, I promise you
I will find it in me,
if ever you throw it down.

Clandestine

I came at last to the crossing-point,
hearing the mandrakes whimper
along a field-edge, ripped
from the furrows and piled up
in grey mouldering heaps with edible
roots, with brassicas;
and all the cafes shut,
the shops boarded up.

A typical day on the frontier.
Imagine my disappointment, though,
on finding the gate demolished,
the guard-hut empty
and the barrier raised to allcomers:
me, with a full set of valid documents
in my pocket; cash;
a cover story that fitted me like a shroud.

Diva

Heavy still with betrayals
she prowls the ramparts,
sniffing the wind;
her gaze a burin
scratching thin images
in the sun's metal:
gods, tribes, running wild
in chariots of vegetation.

It isn't every day
a man can look up
through offal and dried herbs,
letting business slide,
and glimpse annihilation
in the twitch of a hip.

Anchorman

The Towers

Funnelling down through his charm, the disaster
takes shape, exudes an essence: a grey seep
of malodorous plasm, clogging all the space
between us; one travesty after another
hitting the screen, like meteors smashing down
on the porches. A shock evolves in our listening
hands, on our measuring tongues – bitter, sweet,
the gamut of tastes, scents, sentiments, separated
out and inflected through a general narrative.
(His thighs fill the maw of the desk-arch). We're all
at his beck and call, as the litany of preparation
builds: everything will happen if we wait,
will happen again for the first time, in the order
given to it.

Mappa

He needs to believe,
although it's foreign ground
and strange, that a path
leads in, a boat
is waiting somewhere, anywhere,
its sails raised
for him; that the prodigies
are stumbling slowly
in from that wilderness, the crackled edge
of it all, though it all
begins here, this ruck
of stems writhing up,
roots rummaging through stone
ribs and mouths;
that the wound,
niched deep in its jewelled
reliquary, knows who he is, will recognise
his greed,
when the latch is raised
at the primal ceremony.

The Warrior Considers the Tulips

'Hello tulips, I was expecting you.'
Pity about the weather, that sly frost,
but still they came, each perfectly fledged brand,
too perfect, too green. There's nothing mystical
about their slow rush to the magnanimity
                              of appearance –
goblets with shadows in: if we only wait
it happens, but there's no such thing as keeping.
So much required, so little grasped in the hand.
It splits and they make a lunge for us,
as if we were ready or even had anywhere
to put them. It's 'first one to find the monolith',
pure kisses tottering skyward on veins of spittle,
fateful and delicious, needing our defeat
as the prime force, the necessary ground –
blood, fish and bone. And naturally we let them come
since they must come and somebody has to let them.

The Dream
of the Sword

Sliver that commits,
insinuated or blindly
hoiked through the ranged
defences – a flung oath,
a peristyle: meeting no
resistance, it glides on
into marsh, parting reeds,
elaborate oneiric islands;

to a last gunny-sack, sunk
under quilts of mud,
cutting the string.
Stars rush the opening,
crowd the gash, thicken
like spawn. You'd never
believe what it found,
left behind for safe keeping.

Punchinello's Egg

I could almost imagine breaking through from inside it
suddenly, like one of those fully-grown white-pyjamaed
wits in high cones of office, snozzle first
(and snozzle's the word); marotte, confidante,
at the slope,
and everything bearing down like stink:
just one snowy scuff on the flood, one nefarious
stain on the motley. I think my confederates
would gather me up, there would be a place for me
in the stark, undefiled regions.
And there I'd lie
all day in the grass, sniggering at the pilgrims, who'd take
my mask for an outrage, make a small note
in their diaries: 'n.b. beware latitude
such and such, longitude such and such'. Then
many more would stop on their way. I believe
it really could be quite a tourist attraction:
shops, hostelries, chip-vans, stables,
would gather around me,
churches with towers like upturned gnocchi-pots,
a distinct and complex civilization would evolve
quite rapidly around one absurd and invidious
sneer. I would like them to name it after me.
By then, though, I would be irrelevant, just a bloke
in a funny suit, a klutz
with egg on his face.

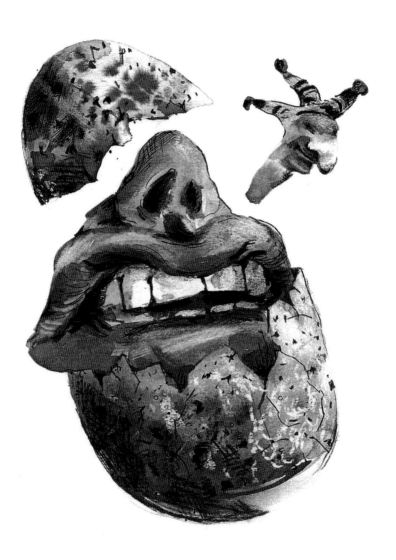

Strange Passage

Just when he thought
he'd shimmied out safely
between the Scylla
and Charybdis of two
incorrigibly overwrought
bramble lynch-mobs, the web
stopped him dead in his tracks...

Much later, if they ever
speak of him, they'll tell
of the warrior who came
to the vineyard, his face
half-covered in a veil
of flames; on his crest –
Arachne, wiggling
her swart limbs.

Anchorman

Fire-Tunnel

Everyone is hungry,
some more than others.
How can he sit still?
They've torn off a haunch,
they've bitten out a chunk.

(Seven kinds of anguish
bloom in the avalanche).

How can he sit still
when the phone goes? It's
only someone gurgling –
'There's no way back,
I've eaten my own map.'

(Seven kinds of absence
bloom in the fire-tunnel).

One day he will rise up
and the desk will rise up with him.

Dancer

Blue-tits prink on bark-mulch.
Over the far house sun macerates the hill,
although a gash resists, high up
where the rib was. Somewhere now she must be striding,
giantess of the uplands, amongst the settlements
flattening her ways, never mind what grew
or was erected - crops,
constituencies, threshing-barns, cathedrals,
stadiums, abodes and bridges. She didn't mean
to break them, it was a dance, she was only dancing,
you see, a shimmy, but the vessels slid
from her grasp, she stumbled and the sun blinded her.
So that's alright then. Not here, not now,
but later and elsewhere some kind of sacrifice
could be in order. Blood is silly though,
is artless, forgets, when daffodils wag their heads.

Petrifactive

Naturally, he crouched there
a long time, barely
daring to twitch
a muscle, until cramp
battened suddenly like a Baltic
winter. He had
to risk it then, raising
his eye carefully
to the shield's rim, but there was
no sign of movement
anywhere: the figure
loomed like a megalith,
eyes flaring out,
mouth gaping in a silent
roar. One arched claw,
theatrically foreshortened,
raking the mist.
Quite simply, she looked
a picture. He couldn't
take his eyes off her.

Victims

They took our cries
and buried them: the roots
went down,
but there were no leaves or fruit.

The roots went down,
straight down, to the nub,
the powerhub; they sucked
at the terrible elixirs.

But there were no leaves
or fruit: when the shoots
came up
they were trampled back.

They hacked
at the roots and the earth bled,
our cries filled the air
again.

The Warrior Considers The Real

There was a certain amount of muck and gore:
the lawn's still heavy with it in the early morning.
La madrugada – it sounds like a cross
between a profane canticle and a woman walking
slowly, very slowly to her last tryst
with someone she couldn't quite save, though she
                                    tried, she tried...
I doubt if my neighbour knew when he spread the grass
and clipped... Happily, the sun mops it dry
occasionally and he lays his towel out like
                                    a flag of leisure,
as if there was nothing missing. Reality
is like that, it doesn't carry very far.
It isn't too much reality we can't bear,
but too little too soon. Some animal's been at
                                    the binbags
again – tins, bacon-rinds: everything turns to mess
in a trice. Which is why we honour the mistaken
no less than the ones who never aspired
                                    in the first place.

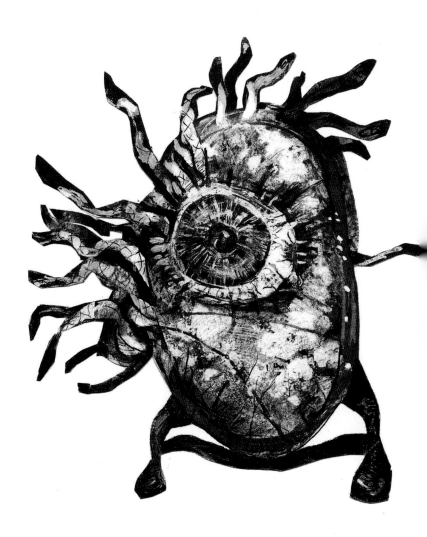

Witness

You cannot turn away
from the shock engraved
on the eyeball; the stare
intaglioed on the lens.

You cannot shut your eye
on the dread that stays
where it is, whether light stabs
or gloom soothes.

The mirror has turned
to stone. There's nothing
to see in the mirror now,
though you cut right through.

Troubadour

This story extends back and forth, back and forth
in time and out of it, one of the fundamental
particles. Whenever she hears a lute
she glows. In the cobbled lane beneath the window
rustle of cloaks and manners, as the queue processes
inward and onward calmly. How odd to think
that somebody stood and looked
but didn't stay. What he'd see was a star,
as if some hooligan once fired an airgun
into a crystal ball: fog everywhere
to begin with, but then that notch, that definitive
rayed singularity he can't take his eyes off,
pulsing and pulsing like the primal strophe.
His body is wrung, is drawn up, just a quivering
string; hardly knowable as the one her shadow
signalled to from the ceiling.

Wanderer

He wanted to punch
right through, but his arm
demurred, his attention wavered; he sat
all day in the square, just listening. He dared
not speak, he knew
that his information
would have betrayed him, finally, as the one
they spoke for, the one
who measured all in the taking:
life and the crimes
of life. Their emotions
prickled on his skin like acid; his bones
grew out and fell through the bench;
but nobody
looked up or thanked him
for his contribution.

The Fix

When he called my name
I could see that map
shimmering down between us.

He turned away
as if turning away
was already setting out.

I can only say
he will never find me
at any of those locations.

The Warrior
and the Oak Trees

Here on the axis mundi
oaks seem to crumble away, and I mean crumble
away: in this field three oaks in four years,
each one more 'venerable' than the last. A high rate
of casualty by any standards. Am I treading too hard?
Or do the owls resent me? One fine
October evening the field was a web:
I picked my way, wherever I glanced out west,
the sun rocked its glittering baby in a cradle
of spun light. All autumn mushrooms spattered the dips
and humps. Probably the field is sick,
but there is a choice if you want to make it:
fall with the trees here, or go home
for good, some kind of celebrity but in a thousand
tiny magnetically incoherent pieces.
Either way the field defines you, the openness you dare.

Resistance (After Lucretius) 2

But if there were no such thing as void
the universe could never be anything but a lump
of solid unyielding matter.
                        On the other hand,
if indestructible bodies did not exist,
solid and indivisible from their first beginnings,
by now the universe would have worn clean away
to nothing, it would have been doomed from the start.

But since it's obvious that neither of those states
accords at present with our personal apprehension
of the world around us, it's safe to say
that there must be bodies, fullnesses between the empty
places, which can neither be broken up by blows
from without, nor pierced, nor shaken nor assailed
in any way. As I've already said,
only if a thing has nothingness within it
can it be crushed or shattered or split in two,
let liquid in, or cold, or the penetrating fire
by which everything is usually eaten up;
and the more each entity holds within it,
the bigger its share of emptiness, the more
it's liable to become a prey to unpleasant
characters wielding swords, hammers and the like.

Campanology

Codes, charms, equations: he's having none of it –
crouched at the lip, or over it, or in that cut
between one point of deliverance and another;
systems, permissions... None of them quite belong
in the way he always needed them to belong
and priced and gave up on, hunkering himself small
in the lea of the parapet, listening for that one
soft, intimate and particular sigh with his name on it.
But still it's difficult to hear anything with those bells
going on and on, still hammering down the reasons
like metal stamps, on top of one another,
each with its glyph, its utterance engraved by hand;
laws, rites, divisions, punching them down methodically –
fortissimo con passione. It's insulting,
why can't they just relax? Are we all so wrong?
One day he will frisk with the flying fishes, leap with
the lambs.

The Miner's Leader

1.
The lamp is primed,
wherever I go
I'm checking for fire-damp.

There'll never be enough light,
there'll never be enough water
hissing in the kettle
where the coal's banked,
or cats in the rocking-chair.

I've seen you flogged, love,
at the sheet-wall; scagged
on a thorn, miles off,
smuts sullying your pallor.
Sorry – I was busy.

Wherever I go
I think of you, whenever
I think of you I'm lost.

2.

All the ones I'd spoken for
had already fallen silent;
all the ones I'd held
in the crook of my arm,
turning them away
from the blast, were already
pierced by the lightning.

Now I hardly recognise
those who my shame lit,
my anger hallowed.
Those who my words sought
have no further use for them.

A man cannot choose
his beneficiaries.

3.
There is a lamp
on the draper's counter.
His shelves are bare.
We've taken all his cloths
and wiped the floor with them.

There is a lamp
in the grocer's. Gutters
curdling with spoil
and cooking-oil. How
do you like them apples?

There is a lamp
in the shoeshop. How many
shoes can a street wear?

There is a lamp
in the sweetshop, a lamp
in the hatshop, a lamp
in the furnitureshop and the ironmonger's
shop,
in the chemist's, the toyshop and the haberdashery,
there is a lamp,
a lamp.

4.
Everything on hold,
but love especially:
we called this the dictatorship
of the proletariat.

One day it would pass
and the wind fade and the smuts
return to the pithead
sheds, and the high tips.

You would pour the tea,
I would open a newspaper.
Perhaps by then
our hands would have stopped shaking.

Love, I was only doing
what I thought best.
If I knew what I knew then
I'd do it again.

But no-one's best is good enough:
rats drool in our litter;
inflammable vapours
bubble in our shirt-seams.

And still they come on,
still the debts are called in,
between Coronation Street
and The Last Supper.

It's none of our business,
none of it is any business
of ours. Come back
from the thorn-bush, I'm waiting.

5.
There is no telling
when the flame will flicker
and turn blue. It could happen
as you open a drawer,
or dabble in the grass
for a prize of eggs.
Whatever's dislodged
or coveted is your enemy.

The Wall

That so much, that anything could have come so far
without a word to say for itself...
No wonder we fret. That wall with its frail inscription,
lichen, ethereal tracery from old downpours,
may be the only monument on the entire map
worth nodding at. A god was there, it left
its terrors propped in a stack.
Its silence sits at the table though it isn't hungry,
smiles at the sacrament, listens to everything we say,
repeating it, though out of sync – there's a slight delay
at all times, a deliquescent blurring effect,
like beauty, worth troubling the mortars for,
worth lying down in the ziggurat of the explosion
for. The point is to make a habit of it,
carry it on your wrist like a charm,
fork out for the poster.

Anchorman

The Camps

By slow increments or in a hurry,
with a retch of metal, concrete, glass
and various kinds of plastic, tearing
into his earphone, cleaving
down, all the way down, down
through the bones, the mandibles,
to the supple tongue, where it sits
waiting for confirmations, consolations
of saliva: here comes the world.
The world? But it doesn't matter, he
is not where the world is, he
is the word delivering itself
in measured tones, concerned
for little children, mothers and fathers,
but mainly mothers and children;
those who wilt in the camps and those
who are taken away at midnight,
taken away and fed to the stones,
by slow increments or in a hurry,
leaving a ditch behind them... That's

where the grammar comes in,
grammar and enunciation,
camera-angle, graphics, that's
where the correspondents come in.
It's not his fault.

Message from Ground Zero

basis of the credit of the
So it goes
the proposed amendments,
Thus
a fund holding a security
rely exclusively on the credit quality
security meets the rule's credit quality
guarantees issued by non-controlled persons
standards. 20
Can we speak of standards?
supra note 6, at nn.8–16 and accompanying
The paper is charred, transparent
(c) (3) (iii) (determination of whether
based exclusively on the credit
subject to guarantees
and frail
(a) (10) (iii) (A)
Notification
controlled

The Guest

Well, who cares if you didn't invite him?
A choice is general, leaves the door open
there where you didn't even know there was a door.
Or a choice, come to that. Claustrophobia
makes the settees get up and walk about,
enquire after relatives, at the poised hour
before the walls fall in. You could at least
have put streamers out, and nibbles, or better still
have engaged the services of a reputable catering firm.
As it is he is ill at ease and therefore bad,
this house looks too much like any other house
in the first risible years of a bodged millennium.
The sword grows small in his hand, but ever more
                                        complex
as sweat arrives, as tedium makes him suck
the glue from the wallpaper. All you can think of
                                        saying
is 'what do you do?' and 'where?' and 'why did
                          you come as me?'

57

Dark

At the very centre of it all, a man
like any other man; at times, a woman;
occasionally both, no doubt – the picture
is never a fixed quantity, there's room
for getting up and putting the tea on, slack
for chewing it over, too; so much depends
on what was said and to whom, what the strangers
settled in the antechamber. He might be beautiful,
truly she might be, but there is no vision
without authority, and none of us knows the booth
where the chit's stamped. A hood is a hood, after all,
in our poor eyes; the grace of the running stag
is not to be found in a cellar, with the candle choked,
(and yet if not there, where?), in a darkness
so remote, so absolute, you can't tell
where chain ends and ominous oedema fattens
about the dumb ring. At the centre of it all
a man or a woman, then, who cannot be seen,
or rarely, and only as somebody we cannot know,
naked and blinking, all their loves abandoned,
and the shires that smelt of hessian,
and the ravishing groves.

Hephaestus:
The Forging

He was the one, of course, it was all
flowing down into him – gold,
silver – every metal under the sun,
alive and smoking, crackling into the furrows.

Copper, bronze, tin – the flame went up
and the house with it, the bushes and the vines
went up with a whoosh! Some error did for them.
Everything would have to pay for the damage done.

Pay and pay well – brass, iron, he
was the one who claimed it, a heraldry
intricate upon his arm, a simulacrum,
wavering, abrupt with heat from the furnace.

Platinum – every metal under the moon.
The shield: a storm in a field, a storm running
across a field running into it, scorched
by the cuff and ready to lie down forgotten.

Knowledge forgotten by the purest artifice.
I made it; I couldn't have known what it was
until I made it, then it was my loss.
He, though, could never have known what it cost,

until his eyes closed and he saw nothing.
Clamped to his breath, his mission, it gripped him shut,
a labyrinth shedding gifts
for those he fell on when the frenzy took him:

dancers and planets, marriages and guitars,
herds, kites, seditions,
shaking the ranks and fuddling the swords
of those ranged against him.

How could I know him, when I saw him pass,
hunched in the shadow of his flawed salvation –
spider crashing through a charred gate
into nowhere?

Also by Lyndon Davies

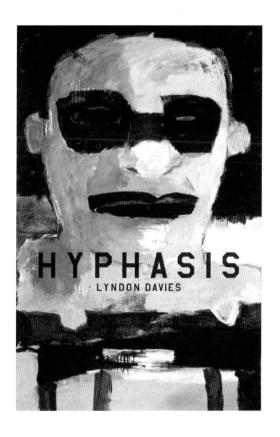

www.parthianbooks.com

More poetry at

PARTHIAN

  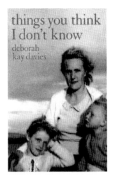

www.parthianbooks.com